HE'S BEEN ON TELEVISION FOR LONGER THAN *ANY OTHER* LATE NIGHT HOST, EXCEPT FOR JOHNNY CARSON. HE'S MADE JOKES OUT OF EVERY DAY SITUATIONS AND HAS MADE HIS WAY INTO THE HEARTS OF MILLIONS, *IF NOT BILLIONS*. WHO IS HE? HE'S *DAVID LETTERMAN!!*
AF241157

DAVID MICHAEL LETTERMAN WAS BORN ON *APRIL 12, 1947* TO HIS PARENTS DOROTHY AND HARRY LETTERMAN. HIS MOTHER, *DOROTHY*, HAS BEEN SEEN ON HIS SHOW A NUMBER OF TIMES OVER THE YEARS, AND HIS FATHER IS CREDITED AS ONE OF THE REASONS DAVID *DOES WHAT HE DOES.*
HE GREW UP NEAR *INDIANAPOLIS* AND HE LOVED PLAYING WITH TOY CARS AND BUILDING *MODEL CARS.*
WHEN DAVID WAS STILL VERY YOUNG, HIS FATHER SUFFERED A *HEART ATTACK* AT THE AGE OF 36. IT DIDN'T STOP HIS DAD FROM CONTINUING TO BE THE *LIFE OF THE PARTY* THOUGH.
DAVID LEARNED, AT A VERY YOUNG AGE, TO *WORK* FOR WHAT HE WANTED. HE WORKED AS A STOCK BOY AT A LOCAL *GROCERY STORE*. IT WAS HIS FIRST TIME WORKING WITH *PRODUCE*, WHICH WOULD COME TO PLAY IN A *BIG* WAY LATER IN LIFE.
HE ATTENDED *BROAD RIPPLE HIGH SCHOOL* IN HIS HOMETOWN, BUT UNFORTUNATELY, HIS GRADES WEREN'T TOO GREAT. HE PROBABLY HAD A *KNACK* FOR COMEDY THEN AND JUST DIDN'T WANT TO PAY ATTENTION IN CLASS.

DAVID WANTED TO ATTEND INDIANA UNIVERSITY, BUT BECAUSE OF HIS LOWER GRADES, HE INSTEAD WENT TO BALL STATE UNIVERSITY IN MUNCIE.
BUT BEING AT BALL STATE DIDN'T CHANGE HIS DESIRE FOR SCHOOLWORK. HE STILL STAYED AN AVERAGE STUDENT, NOT PAYING MUCH ATTENTION IN CLASS.
IT DIDN'T MATTER. HE JOINED THE SIGMA CHI FRATERNITY...
WORKING ALONGSIDE HIS BROTHERS IN THE FRATERNITY TO BECOME A PART OF THE CAMPUS.
HE GRADUATED FROM BALL STATE IN 1969, AND IT'S SAFE TO SAY THAT HIS TIME WITH SIGMA CHI HELPED HIM TO FIND HIS WAY FROM AN AVERAGE C STUDENT TO SOMETHING MORE.

DAVID'S FIRST TASTE FOR BROADCASTING STARTED IN COLLEGE WHEN HE READ THE *NEWS* AT BALL STATE'S *COLLEGE RADIO* STATION. HE DIDN'T LAST LONG THOUGH (AND UNFORTUNATELY, A LOT OF HIS WORK ENDS THE *SAME WAY*)...
HE WAS *FIRED* BECAUSE OF HIS *IRREVERENT* WAYS AND THE WAY HE TREATED CLASSICAL MUSIC. NOT EVERYONE UNDERSTANDS DAVID'S COMEDY, AND IT SEEMS THAT'S BEEN A STAPLE OF HIS LIFE.
IT WASN'T UNTIL 1969 THAT DAVID FIGURED OUT WHAT HE WANTED TO DO AND WHO HE WANTED TO BE. WHILE WATCHING THE *PAUL DIXON* SHOW, DAVID SEEMED TO BE SUDDENLY STRUCK WITH INSPIRATION, AND HE CREDITS PAUL DIXON FOR IT.
THAT'S REALLY WHAT I WANT TO DO!
AND SOON AFTER FINDING HIS CALLING, DAVID DOVE IN HEADFIRST. HE STARTED AS A RADIO *TALK SHOW HOST* AND THEN AS A WEATHERMAN AND LOCAL NEWS ANCHOR IN *INDIANAPOLIS* AS WELL. THIS WAS HIS BIG BREAK AND WHERE HE WOULD FIRST FIND HIS AUDIENCE.
IT WAS HERE THAT HIS *STRANGE COMEDIC STYLE* WOULD COME OUT IN FULL BLOOM. HE MADE *WILD* PREDICTIONS ABOUT THE WEATHER, MADE UP TOWNS AND CITIES, AND JOKED ABOUT *EVERYTHING*.
58

IN 1975, HE DECIDED TO MOVE TO LOS ANGELES AFTER BEING URGED BY HIS WIFE MICHELLE AND HIS SIGMA CHI BROTHERS TO MOVE OUT AND BECOME A COMEDY WRITER. HE AND MICHELLE WERE ON THEIR WAY...

AND WHEN THEY MADE IT, DAVID JUMPED IN HEADFIRST, WRITING MATERIAL FOR OTHER COMICS LIKE JIMMIE WALKER AND WRITING HIS OWN MATERIAL THAT HE WOULD THEN PERFORM ON STAGE AS WELL.

DAVID ALSO FOUND TIME TO ACT ON TELEVISION, TAKING ROLES ON SHOWS SUCH AS MARY (FEATURING MARY TYLER MOORE), AND A GUEST SPOT ON MORK AND MINDY OPPOSITE ROBIN WILLIAMS...

6

HE EVEN MADE APPEARANCES ON GAME SHOWS FROM THE 1970S LIKE THE GONG SHOW AND $20,000 PYRAMID, AMONG OTHERS. BUT HIS BIG BREAK WOULDN'T COME UNTIL A FEW YEARS LATER WHEN TALENT SCOUTS NOTICED HIM AND DECIDED TO BRING HIM ON A HUGE LATE-NIGHT TALK SHOW. YOU MAY HAVE HEARD OF IT...

14

$50

THE TONIGHT SHOW STARRING JOHNNY CARSON! DAVID WOULD BECOME A REGULAR GUEST ON JOHNNY'S SHOW...
DOING HIS STAND UP ROUTINE THAT MADE HIM ONE OF JOHNNY CARSON'S FAVORITE GUESTS...
EVEN GOING SO FAR AS TO SOMETIMES BE A GUEST HOST WHEN JOHNNY WAS AWAY. IT WAS THE BIGGEST STEP IN DAVID'S CAREER, AND HIS TIME WORKING ALONGSIDE AND BEING ON JOHNNY'S SHOW INFLUENCED DAVID'S CAREER MORE THAN ANY OTHERS.

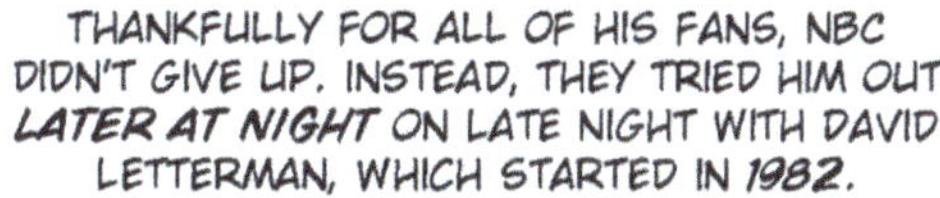

BEGINNING IN *1980*, NBC ATTEMPTED TO GIVE HIM HIS OWN SHOW, IRONICALLY CALLED THE DAVID LETTERMAN SHOW, THAT WAS A *CRITICAL DARLING* BUT A *RATINGS FLOP*.

THANKFULLY FOR ALL OF HIS FANS, NBC DIDN'T GIVE UP. INSTEAD, THEY TRIED HIM OUT *LATER AT NIGHT* ON LATE NIGHT WITH DAVID LETTERMAN, WHICH STARTED IN *1982*.

IT WAS AN EARLY MORNING COMEDY SHOW THAT UNFORTUNATELY, *NO ONE WATCHED*.

IT AIRED AFTER JOHNNY CARSON AND WAS A *HUGE* SUCCESS WITH *COLLEGE STUDENTS* (SOUNDS LIKE SOMEONE ELSE WHO HAD A LATE NIGHT SHOW ON NBC, DOESN'T IT?).

MOST OF HIS COMEDY *STAPLES* STARTED ON THIS PROGRAM.

HIS *TOP TEN LISTS*, *STUPID PET* AND HUMAN TRICKS, DROPPING THINGS OFF THE ROOF TO SEE HOW THEY SMASHED, AND OTHER *RIDICULOUS* COMEDY BITS EITHER BEGAN OR CONTINUED HERE.

IT GAVE HIM A RECURRING *FANBASE* AND MADE HIM INTO A KNOWN COMEDIC *ENTITY*.

ANOTHER OF HIS STAPLES WAS THE *UNPREDICTABILITY* OF THE SHOW. HIS GUEST INTERVIEWS WOULD OFTEN TAKE STRANGE, HILARIOUS *TURNS*.

SOME INCLUDED *SHOUTING* MATCHES, GUESTS STORMING OFF THE STAGE, OR EVEN *WRESTLING KNOCKDOWNS*.

LATE NIGHT WOULDN'T LAST *FOREVER*, THOUGH, AND IN *1992*, THE CURTAINS CLOSED AFTER JOHNNY CARSON *RETIRED* AND DAVID DECIDED TO MOVE TO *CBS*. THERE HAS BEEN A LOT OF TALK ON THE MOVE AND WHAT *CAUSED* IT.

MOST FANS BELIEVED HE WOULD *TAKE OVER* THE TONIGHT SHOW, AND FOR ALL INTENTS AND PURPOSES, HE WAS *CARSON'S PICK* TO TAKE THE ROLE. WHEN NBC CHOSE *LENO*, LETTERMAN OPTED TO LEAVE AND *CREATED HIS OWN SHOW* ON CBS.

SO IN 1993, THE LATE SHOW WITH DAVID LETTERMAN PREMIERED ON CBS, GOING ON AGAINST THE TONIGHT SHOW WITH JAY LENO. THE SHOW WAS NOT IDENTICAL TO HIS LATE NIGHT SHOW, BUT IT DID RETAIN MOST OF HIS UNPREDICTABILITY.
PAUL SHAFFER CONTINUED ON AS BANDLEADER BUT GOT A LARGE BAND IN THE PROCESS, DAVID GAINED A HIGHER SALARY AND A BETTER TIME SLOT, AND SOME OF HIS LATE NIGHT TRADEMARKS HAD TO BE CHANGED EVER SO SLIGHTLY TO AVOID COPYRIGHT INFRINGEMENT.
THIS WAS THE BIRTH OF THE CBS MAILBAG, THE LATE SHOW TOP TEN, AND THE CONTINUATION OF STUPID HUMAN AND STUPID PET TRICKS. IT WAS A RATINGS AND CRITICAL SUCCESS.

IN 1995, DAVID BROUGHT HIS IRREVERENT COMEDY TO AN EVEN BIGGER TELEVISED EVENT, THE ACADEMY AWARDS.
IT DIDN'T GO SO WELL.
A LOT OF HIS JOKES JUST DIDN'T HIT THE MARK, INCLUDING A LONG INTRODUCTION BETWEEN UMA THURMAN AND OPRAH WINFREY.
UMA!
OPRAH!
IT WAS UNFORTUNATE, AND SOME BELIEVE IT MAY HAVE AFFECTED THE RATINGS ON HIS LATE SHOW AS WELL, BUT DAVID ALWAYS BOUNCED BACK.
HE MADE JOKES ABOUT THE EXPERIENCE. HE MADE LIGHT OF IT. HE EVEN PLAYED AGAINST IT DURING THE OSCARS WHEN BILLY CRYSTAL HOSTED.
BUT IN SPITE OF ALL THE BAD PUBLICITY AND THE BAD CRITICAL REVIEWS, THE ACADEMY LOVED HIS PERFORMANCE AND EVEN ASKED HIM ON AT LEAST ONE OCCASION TO COME BACK AND HOST AGAIN.

IN 2000, FOLLOWING A ROUTINE CHECK-UP, IT WAS FOUND THAT DAVID'S HEART WAS *SEVERELY CONSTRICTED* AND NEEDED AN EMERGENCY *QUINTUPLE BYPASS.*

HEART ISSUES HAD *ALWAYS* BEEN IN HIS HEAD, AFTER HIS FATHER HAD SURVIVED ONE HEART ATTACK AT THE AGE OF 36 ONLY TO SUFFER A *SECOND* HEART ATTACK AT THE AGE OF 57 AND PASS AWAY. DAVID WAS ALMOST 53 WHEN HIS HEART ISSUE WAS DISCOVERED.

DURING HIS RECOVERY, INSTEAD OF JUST PLAYING *RERUNS* OR TAKING THE SHOW OFF THE AIR ENTIRELY, DAVID INTRODUCED SOMETHING THAT HADN'T BEEN SEEN IN LATE NIGHT TALK SHOWS SINCE *CARSON* HAD RETIRED...

THE *GUEST HOST.*

BILL COSBY* WAS HIS FIRST GUEST HOST WHILE DAVID WAS TAKING TIME TO RECOVER, AND MANY OF THE GUEST HOSTS OPTED *NOT* TO USE HIS DESK TO INTERVIEW GUESTS, USING *MAKE-SHIFT* DESKS OR USING THE COUCHES INSTEAD.

AND WHEN DAVID RETURNED TO THE SHOW, HE BROUGHT ALONG THE *NURSES* AND *DOCTORS* WHO SAVED HIS LIFE, MAKING JOKES ABOUT THEM SEEING HIS INSIDES OR SEEING HIM NAKED, AND IN THE END, BEING *GENUINE* AND *GRACIOUS* FOR THEM SAVING HIM.

BUT JUST BECAUSE THEY SAVED HIS LIFE, IT DIDN'T STOP DAVID FROM CONTINUING TO *CRACK JOKES.*

A FEW YEARS LATER, WHEN HE WAS DIAGNOSED WITH SHINGLES, DAVID TOOK SOME TIME OFF FROM THE SHOW AND BROUGHT BACK THE GUEST HOSTS AGAIN, THIS TIME USING PEOPLE LIKE BILL COSBY, VINCE VAUGHN, WILL FERRELL, AND HIS PAL PAUL SHAFFER.
FOR A TIME, HE INCORPORATED GUEST HOSTS ON FRIDAY SHOWS.

OVER THE NEXT FEW YEARS, HE WOULD MAKE WAVES ONCE MORE BY DECIDING TO *STAY WITH CBS* INSTEAD OF JUMP SHIP. THE OPPORTUNITY CAME TO HIM IN BOTH *2002* AND *2006* TO LEAVE CBS FOR *ABC*, BUT HE STAYED WITH CBS ON BOTH OCCASIONS.
IN 2002, HE DIDN'T WANT TO TAKE OVER THE TIME SLOT OF *TED KOPPEL'S NIGHTLINE* OUT OF *RESPECT* FOR KOPPEL AND BECAUSE HE WAS HAPPY AT CBS. HIS HAPPINESS WITH CBS IS WHY HE DECIDED TO STAY, *AGAIN*, IN 2006.
I'M THRILLED TO BE CONTINUING ON AT CBS. AT MY AGE YOU REALLY DON'T WANT TO HAVE TO LEARN A NEW *COMMUTE*.

THIS *LOYALTY* TO FRIENDS IS SOMETHING DAVID HAS SHOWN FOR YEARS, INCLUDING WITH HIS FRIEND AND *MENTOR*, JOHNNY CARSON. IN SPITE OF WHAT HAPPENED WITH TONIGHT SHOW...
JOHNNY AND DAVID *REMAINED* FRIENDS.

JOHNNY'S *LAST* TELEVISION APPEARANCE CAME DURING A 1994 EPISODE OF THE LATE SHOW TAPED IN LOS ANGELES, THOUGH JOHNNY *COULDN'T SPEAK* AS THE AUDIENCE CLAPPED FOR *SO LONG* THAT HE DIDN'T HAVE A CHANCE TO.
(OR HE HAD *LARYNGITIS*, WHICH HAS ALSO BEEN BLAMED FOR HIS INABILITY TO SPEAK AT THE TIME).

IT WAS ALSO REVEALED THAT JOHNNY WOULD *SEND JOKES* TO DAVID FROM TIME TO TIME, AND ANYTIME HE READ ONE, DAVID WOULD DO THE JOHNNY CARSON *GOLF SWING* AFTER. JOHNNY LOVED IT EVERY TIME HIS FRIEND WOULD READ HIS JOKES...

AND ON DAVID'S FIRST SHOW FOLLOWING JOHNNY CARSON'S DEATH, *ALL* OF THE JOKES IN THE OPENING MONOLOGUE WERE REVEALED TO HAVE BEEN *WRITTEN BY CARSON*. IT WAS A FITTING *TRIBUTE* FROM ONE FRIEND TO ANOTHER.

IN 2005, A LONGSTANDING *FEUD* BETWEEN *OPRAH WINFREY* AND DAVID LETTERMAN HAD ENDED. FOLLOWING THE UMA-OPRAH OSCARS INCIDENT, THE TWO BARELY TALKED FOR *10 YEARS*, UNTIL OPRAH AGREED TO BE A GUEST ON DAVID'S SHOW.
DAVID CALLED IT THE *SUPER BOWL OF LOVE*, AND IT WAS THE FIRST TIME SHE WAS ON HIS SHOW SINCE HE HAD MOVED FROM NBC.

IN 2007, SHE EXTENDED THE *SAME GRACE*, HAVING HIM ON HER SHOW WHICH WAS FILMED AT *MADISON SQUARE GARDEN*.

BUT IT WASN'T THE *ONLY TIME* THESE TWO WOULD BE SEEN TOGETHER. ALSO IN 2007, OPRAH AND DAVID FILMED A LATE SHOW *PROMO* WHICH SHOWED DURING THE 2007 SUPER BOWL WHERE THEY WATCHED THE GAME TOGETHER, WEARING *OPPOSING TEAM JERSEYS*.

AND THE SAME JOKE WOULD BE USED AGAIN IN *2010*, WHEN OPRAH WOULD BE SEATED ON THE COUCH BETWEEN LETTERMAN AND *LENO*, FOR ANOTHER PROMO FOR THE LATE SHOW, SHOWN DURING THE SUPER BOWL. THIS JOKE WAS *LETTERMAN'S IDEA*, GOING SO FAR AS TO HAVE LENO SNEAK INTO THE SULLIVAN THEATER *IN DISGUISE*.

BETWEEN 2007 AND 2008, THE LATE SHOW WENT OFF THE AIR DUE TO THE WRITERS GUILD OF AMERICA'S STRIKE. IT WAS A SHORT-LIVED STRIKE FOR HIS SHOW, ONLY 8 WEEKS, BECAUSE OF WHAT HIS PRODUCTION COMPANY WAS ABLE TO DO.
HIS COMPANY, WORLDWIDE PANTS, WAS ABLE TO MAKE AN INDIVIDUAL AGREEMENT WITH THE WGA, AND GOT HIS SHOW BACK ON THE AIR ON JANUARY 2, 2008. IT WAS THE FIRST COMPANY TO MAKE SUCH A DEAL AND SET THE BAR FOR EVERYONE ELSE.
WRITERS GUILD OF AMERICA ON STRIKE
GUILD OF AMERICA ON STRIKE
AND DURING THE STRIKE, SIMILAR TO CONAN O'BRIEN'S OFF-THE-AIR BEARD, DAVID GREW A BEARD IN SOLIDARITY WITH THE WRITERS. IT DIDN'T LAST LONG THOUGH...

DAVID HAD CREATED HIS OWN PRODUCTION COMPANY, WORLDWIDE PANTS, WHICH PRODUCED HIS SHOW AND MANY OTHERS INCLUDING EVERYBODY LOVES RAYMOND, THE LATE LATE SHOW AND THE NBC SERIES ED.
THEY EVEN PRODUCED THEIR FIRST FEATURE FILM, STRANGERS WITH CANDY, BASED ON THE CULT COMEDY CENTRAL SERIES STARRING AMY SEDARIS AND STEPHEN COLBERT.
AND IN LATE 2007, WORLDWIDE PANTS WAS THE FIRST COMPANY TO INDEPENDENTLY NEGOTIATE A CONTRACT WITH THE WRITERS GUILD OF AMERICA, EAST, WHICH ALLOWED LETTERMAN AND CRAIG FERGUSON TO GO BACK ON THE AIR, WITH THEIR WRITERS. THE STRIKE CONTINUED AGAINST OTHER PRODUCTION COMPANIES AND NETWORKS AND OTHERS, BUT WHERE EVERYONE ELSE HAD FAILED, LETTERMAN'S COMPANY HAD SUCCEEDED AND SET THE BAR FOR OTHERS TO FOLLOW.
HE EVEN HAS HIS OWN PRIVATE FOUNDATION, THE AMERICAN FOUNDATION FOR COURTESY AND GROOMING. HE'S USED THE FOUNDATION TO DONATE MILLIONS OF DOLLARS TO CHARITIES, NON-PROFIT ORGANIZATIONS, UNIVERSITIES, AND EVEN TO THE SALVATION ARMY AND THE AMERICAN CANCER SOCIETY. HE'S NOT AFRAID TO GIVE BACK...

IN 2007, DAVID LETTERMAN VISITED BALL STATE IN MUNCIE, INDIANA, FOR THE DEDICATION OF THE DAVID LETTERMAN COMMUNICATION AND MEDIA BUILDING.
DAVID GAVE A SPEECH IN FRONT OF THE STATE-OF-THE-ART CENTER, DETAILING HIS COLLEGE STRUGGLES AND TALKING ABOUT HIS FAMILY. BUT NO MATTER HOW HEARTFELT, THERE WERE ALWAYS JOKES TO BE HAD.
LL STATE UNIVERSITY   EDUCATION REDEFINED
IF REASONABLE PEOPLE CAN PUT MY NAME ON A $21 MILLION BUILDING, ANYTHING IS POSSIBLE.

DAVID HAS ALSO LIVED A RICH LIFE IN THE *FICTIONAL* REALMS AS WELL. HE'S APPEARED IN *COMIC BOOKS* FEATURING *THE AVENGERS* AND *BATMAN*.

HE'S MET *THE SIMPSONS* IN A COUCH GAG FROM THEIR SHOW AS WELL (THAT'S *TWO* FORMER LATE NIGHT HOSTS WHO'VE MET THE SIMPSONS).

SOMETHING DAVID PROBABLY CONSIDERS TO BE ONE OF HIS *BIGGEST* MOMENTS IN HIS LIFE WOULD BE WORKING ALONGSIDE HIS FRIEND *WARREN ZEVON* FOR THE SONG *HIT SOMEBODY*. HE HAS WORKED WITH MUSIC AND SHOWN HIS LOVE OF MUSIC FOR ALL THE YEARS HE'S BEEN ON TELEVISION, BUT HE WAS ALWAYS A *FRIEND* AND *FAN* TO WARREN ZEVON.

AND HE'S PLAYED *HIMSELF* A NUMBER OF TIMES AS WELL. HE HAD A ROLE IN THE FILM *PRIVATE PARTS*, STARRING *HOWARD STERN*, AND HE WAS HIMSELF IN THE MOVIE *MAN ON THE MOON*, ABOUT THE LIFE STORY OF *ANDY KAUFMAN*.

OVER THE YEARS, DAVID HAS FOUND *LOVE* ON A NUMBER OF OCCASIONS.

HE WAS MARRIED TO *MICHELLE COOK* FROM 1969 TO 1977, AND THEN HAD A LONG-TERM RELATIONSHIP WITH *MERRILL MARKOE* WHO WAS A *PRODUCER* AND *WRITER* FOR HIS LATE NIGHT SHOW. SINCE 1986, HE HAS BEEN WITH HIS CURRENT WIFE *REGINA LASKO*, THOUGH THE TWO HAVE ONLY BEEN MARRIED SINCE 2009.

IN 2003, REGINA AND DAVID WELCOMED THEIR SON, *HARRY JOSEPH LETTERMAN*, INTO THE WORLD, NAMED AFTER DAVID'S FATHER. WITH ALL THE LOVE THEY SHARED, WHY SOMEONE WOULD TRY TO GO AFTER THEM IS *SHAMEFUL*, BUT IN 2005, POLICE DISCOVERED A *KIDNAPPING PLOT* TO TAKE HARRY AND *RANSOM* HIM OFF TO DAVID LETTERMAN FOR *$5 MILLION*.

ILLINOIS

THANKFULLY, CHARGES WERE BROUGHT TO A *HOUSE PAINTER* WHO HAD WORKED FOR LETTERMAN PREVIOUSLY, AND DAVID'S SON HAD *NEVER* BEEN KIDNAPPED.

IN 2009, IT WAS REVEALED ON HIS PROGRAM THAT HE WAS THE VICTIM OF AN EXTORTION ATTEMPT. SOMEONE WAS THREATENING TO REVEAL SEXUAL RELATIONSHIPS HE HAD HAD WITH FEMALE EMPLOYEES IN THE PAST, RELATIONSHIPS HE WOULD THEN CONFIRM.
HE WORKED ALONGSIDE THE POLICE TO PERFORM A STING ON THE PERPETRATOR OF THIS ATTEMPT, WHO WAS THEN ARRESTED BY THE POLICE AND REVEALED TO BE A PRODUCER FOR ANOTHER CBS SERIES.

BECAUSE OF THIS EXTORTION ATTEMPT, HIS DIRTY LAUNDRY WAS BEING AIRED ON NATIONAL TELEVISION FOR ALL TO SEE. ALLEGATIONS WERE MADE AND SECRET AFFAIRS WERE ANNOUNCED BETWEEN DAVID AND FORMER EMPLOYEES AND ASSISTANTS, BUT DAVID DIDN'T HIDE BEHIND THE ALLEGATIONS. HE CONFRONTED THEM AND TOOK THEM HEAD ON. HE APOLOGIZED TO HIS WIFE AND HIS STAFF, AND WAS HONEST AND UPFRONT ABOUT WHAT HE HAD DONE.
HE BEGGED FORGIVENESS, AND HIS AUDIENCE AND STAFF SEEMINGLY GAVE THAT TO HIM. HE HAD MADE A MISTAKE, BUT IN APOLOGIZING AND NOT CONFESSING, HE MADE AMENDS MUCH QUICKER AND REGAINED THE TRUST OF MILLIONS.
IT SHOWED THAT ALL THE AWARDS AND ADULATION HE HAD RECEIVED OVER THE YEARS WEREN'T A SHAM, IT SHOWED THAT THEY HADN'T GONE TO HIS HEAD. IT SHOWED THAT HE WAS STILL HUMAN AND WOULD STILL MAKE MISTAKES.

IN SPITE OF HIS MISTAKES, DAVID LETTERMAN IS STILL ON TOP OF HIS GAME. HE'S STILL HILARIOUS, HE'S STILL A COMEDIC GENIUS AND A CULT FAVORITE, AND HIS COMEDY STILL TICKLES THE FUNNY BONES OF MILLIONS OF PEOPLE EVERY SINGLE WEEKNIGHT.
HE'S MADE MISTAKES AND HE'S PAID FOR THEM, BUT IN MOVING PAST THEM AND BEING OPEN ON THE AIR, HE'S TAKEN A STANCE THAT VERY FEW PEOPLE IN THE LIMELIGHT DO.
HE'S SHOWING HIMSELF, WARTS AND ALL, TO HIS VIEWERS, ASKING US TO ACCEPT HIM THE WAY THAT HE IS. AND WE DO. WE DO BECAUSE DAVID LETTERMAN IS A FIXTURE OF LATE NIGHT COMEDY, AND WE'RE NOT READY TO SEE HIM GO YET.
NOUMIER TAWILAH 2012

CW Cooke — Writer

Noumier Tawilah — Penciler

Noumier Tawilah — Colorist

David Hopkins — Letterer

Noumier Tawilah — Cover

Darren G. Davis
Publisher

Jason Schultz
Vice President

Jarred Weisfeld
Literary Manager

Kailey Marsh
Entertainment Manager

Maggie Jessup
Publicity

Darren G. Davis
Editor

Warren Montgomery
Production

www.bluewaterprod.com

PORTLAND'S

CONCERT

HALL

TOC
CONCERT HALL